Swim, Allison, Swim!

Featuring Allison the Green Sea Turtle

Written by Sheryl Jones

Illustrated by Debbie Smith

PALOMA BOOKS   ASHLAND, OREGON

Swim, Allison, Swim!
©2015 Sheryl Jones

Published by Paloma Books
(An imprint of L&R Publishing, LLC)

All rights reserved. No part of this publication may be reproduced or used in any form or by any means, graphic, electronic or mechanical, including photocopying, recording, taping, or information and retrieval systems without written permission of the publisher.

Paloma Books
PO Box 3531
Ashland, OR 97520
www.palomabooks.com

Front and Back Cover Illustrations by Debbie Smith

ISBN: 978-1-55571-776-6

Printed and bound in the United States of America

Dedicated to the Staff
and Volunteers
at Sea Turtle Inc.
And to a Brave Little Green Sea Turtle
Who Just Keeps on Swimming!

Once upon a time there was a green sea turtle named Allison. She lived in a tank.

She had only one flipper.
A shark ate the other three.
Poor Allison!

Allison does not care.
She does what all sea turtles do.
She keeps swimming!

But with just one flipper,
Allison can swim only in circles!

Some people who loved Allison made her a new flipper that fit on her back.

Now Allison can swim in a straight line.
Everyone smiled!
Swim, Allison, Swim!

A big man with a big belly
and big sunglasses watched Allison swim.

And he smiled.
Swim, Allison, Swim!

A little girl who was mad at her brother watched Allison swim.

Pretty soon she smiled!
Swim, Allison, Swim!

A lady with a cane
watched Allison swim.

She smiled and waved her cane in the air.
Swim, Allison, Swim!

Three teenage girls talked and talked on their cell phones while they watched Allison swim.

Then they stopped talking and smiled.
Swim, Allison, Swim!

A grumpy old man who didn't want
to come see the turtles watched Allison.

Pretty soon he smiled, too.
Swim, Allison, Swim!

An eighth grade boy who wantedto be a doctor when he grew up watched Allison.

He smiled and dreamed how he would help people like Allison. Swim, Allison, Swim!

A young soldier with a new leg and a new arm watched Allison. He watched and watched.

Then he saluted and smiled—
a great BIG smile!
Swim, Allison, Swim!

Everyone who watches Allison swim,
smiles and smiles and smiles!
Swim, Allison, Swim!

If you want to see Allison swim, come visit her and all the other sea turtles at Sea Turtle Inc., 6617 Padre Blvd., South Padre Island, Texas or visit our web site at www.seaturtleinc.org.

Be sure and look for all of these fun books about the turtles at Sea Turtle Inc.

Smile and Say, "Lettuce!"

Fred, the Lopsided Loggerhead

The Turtle Corral

Swim, Allison, Swim!

CPSIA information can be obtained
at www.ICGtesting.com
Printed in the USA
JSHW011948260321
12968JS00002B/6